Kids Read and Write
Japanese Tanka

by VA Rivera

Introduce kids ages 8 and older to poetry with simple Japanese Tanka.

Discover themes and syllable patterns. Kids are encouraged to
use model poems to write their own. Great for parents, teachers, or
anyone helping kids learn an appreciation for the art of poetry.

Publishing Services by:
Telemachus Press, LLC
7652 Sawmill Road, Suite 304
Dublin, Ohio 43016

ISBN: 978-1-965121-19-1
Version: 20250528

Introduction: What is a Japanese Tanka?

Welcome to the wonderful world of Japanese Tanka! The word tanka means "short song." Japanese Tanka poems are short poems that were first written in Japan during the 17th Century.

Japanese Tanka poems do not rhyme. Tanka poems are written in one unbroken sentence. Tanka uses much description. Tanka in the English language has a total of five lines.

The first line has 5 syllables.
The second line has 7 syllables.
The third line has 5 syllables.
The fourth line has 7 syllables.
The fifth line has 7 syllables.

Japanese Tankas are usually about a personal experience or observation. The poet writes about something that happened to the poet or something the poet saw. The poet writes with strong feeling or emotion. Poets use their creativity and imagination! And that, my friends, is part of what makes writing poetry so much fun!

Read Kids Read and Write Japanese Tanka to help you learn how Tankas are written. The Tankas in this book are inspired by poems written by many talented elementary students with whom the author has had the pleasure teaching. I hope readers will feel inspired to write your own!

Play with words. Use your senses. Use your emotions. Use your wonderful imagination to create your own Japanese Tanka poems. Remember to have fun!

Chapter 1 Seasons Japanese Tanka Poems

Each new season is magical.

Autumn amazes when leaves on trees turn brightly cheerful colors. Winter brings billions of snow crystals – no one snowflake is like the other, just like people. Spring brings sunshine's warm rays on our faces. When Summer fun comes, we shed our sweaters and coats for sunglasses and swimsuits!

Seasons make life interesting!

Here are Seasons Tanka poems for you to enjoy!

Brisk Day

Yellow, orange, red,

and brown tumble to the ground

in chilly autumn

air while mothers search for gloves

and children button their coats

Skiers on Hills

Serenity's new

name gracefully whispers still

as skiers on hills

slide through transparent blankets

of ice like layers of light

Spring

awakening sun

revealing hidden gardens

whose crawling creatures

disturbed by roaring mowers

search for new hiding places

Summer Heat

day dawn awakens
birds taking curtain calls on
my windowsill peck
seeds left for morning sunlight
before the day's heat sets in

In Chapter 1 you learned about Seasons Japanese Tanka Poems. Now it's your turn to write one of your own! First choose your favorite season to write about. Remember to use the 5/7/5/7/7 pattern of syllables! Share your Tanka with a friend, an adult you know, or a teacher.

Chapter 2 Animals Japanese Tanka Poems

Most people have experiences with their pets. But people around the world enjoy the company of many different types of animals. Animals depend on us to take care of them and be friends. Animals want to be loved just like people.

Read the following Animal Tanka poems.

Pony Tanka

I can't wait because
mom says she is getting me
a pony when she
wins the New York State million
dollar lottery some day

Puppy Tanka Poem

I wish I were a
puppy cute and cuddly
wrapped in a soft warm
blanket on the master bed
dreaming of chewing on an

old pair of smelly
sneakers or nibbling my
favorite Kibble
then running after squirrels
in a grassy field

Kitty's Crunchy Ear

Cauliflower ear

makes her look tough, bully-on-

the-block tough, but kitty just

needs lovin' with that don't-mess-

with-me cauliflower ear

In Chapter 2 different animals were the subjects of Tanka poems. Think of an animal about whom you would like to write a Japanese Tanka poem. Maybe it's your pet at home. Maybe a zoo animal you once saw. Or perhaps a favorite animal of your daydreams. Choose an animal as the subject of your very own animal Tanka poem. Write and share with someone, perhaps a parent, friend, or teacher.

Chapter 3 Clothing Tanka poems

Who would ever guess a Japanese Tanka poem could be written about the clothes you wear. But yes, you can! Look at the following examples of Tanka poems about clothes. Think about which article of clothing about which you would like to write a Japanese Tanka poem!

New Shoes

I told my mom a
little pinch would not hurt
my toes especially since
the new shoes matched my outfit
though my feet screamed at me, NO!

What Shoes?

I don't like shoes on
hot rainy days I'd rather
wiggle my toes in
wet squishy mud while letting
the grass tidy up my feet

Mom calls out take care
my dear, do not muss your shoes
I grin and think, no
need to worry, took care of
that what shoes, I say, what shoes?

Writer's Sweater

My hand is cramped, my
notebook is empty, and my
pencil keeps breaking,
I've had writers block for days,
so, I put on my lucky

writer's sweater and
start again with my hand at
ease, my pencil sharp,
I scr-ibb-le one new idea
and thank my lucky sweater

In Chapter 3 different articles of clothing was the subject of Tanka poems. Think which article of clothing you would like to write about in a Japanese Tanka poem.

Maybe your favorite sneakers. Maybe a fun summer shirt. Or perhaps a fancy outfit for a special occasion. Choose one as the subject of your very own animal Tanka poem.

Remember to use the 5/7/5 pattern of syllables! Write and share with someone, perhaps a parent, friend, or teacher.

Chapter 4 Food Tanka Poems

All people eat to live. Some people live to eat. Almost everyone can think of a favorite food. Maybe it's a delicious meal you help your family cook, maybe a favorite treat, maybe something yummy you eat only on special occasions. Think about one or some of your favorite foods to eat and enjoy the following Food Tanka poems.

Tuna

Mayonnaise is a
treat on tuna sandwiches
with parsley and a
crunchy celery surprise
on pumpernickel bagels

Sandwich Song

Triangle fun to
eat bologna sandwiches
with mayonnaise or
sometimes mustard or alone
on slices of Wonder Bread.

PB &J

I used to sing the
peanut butter and jelly
song when I was a
kid but the sticky sweet words
stuck to the roof of my mouth.

Jalapeños

Deli sliced ham makes

for a fine sub but do not

add jalapeños,

or you'll need a gallon of

whole milk to cool the fire

Bellyache

chips salsa popcorn
pretzels soda pop party
games giggling large
pepperoni cheese pizza
fudge brownies ice cream cake, burp!

In Chapter 4 you read fun Japanese Tanka poems about favorite foods. Now it's your turn to write one of your own! First choose a food to write about. Any food that comes to mind. Remember to use the 5/7/5 pattern of syllables! Share your Tanka with a friend, an adult you know, or a teacher!

Chapter 5 Earth Around Us

Humans live on a beautiful planet called Earth. Earth is known as a blue planet because 71% of the planet is covered by water. Much of the vegetation on Earth is green. And there is a rainbow of many colors everywhere.

Our responsibility to Earth is to take care of her while we marvel at her beauty. The following Japanese Tanka Poems speak of glorious nature around us.

Snowy Mountain Tale

Jay crosses darkened
gray sky almost unnoticed,
red bird soars brightly
against mountain top's snow white
against mountain top's pure white

Wee Caterpillar

Fuzzy creature creeps

along, climbs the greenery

wall, with every

footstep nib-bl-ing, do tell

us how many footsteps - all.

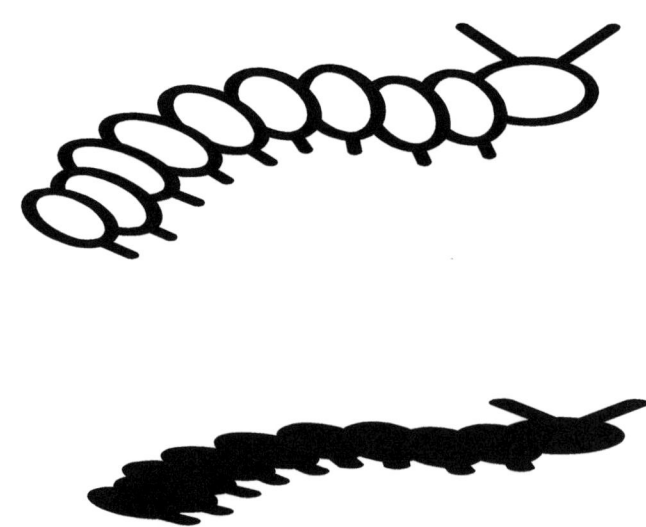

Bird Sanctuary

flaps down, smooth landing

splendid perch on fingertips

a nod and a peck

snatching black sunflower seeds

and my heart, quick as a wink

In Chapter 5 you read Japanese Tanka Poems about nature found on the Earth. Now imagine in your mind a picture of a nature place or thing on Earth that you would like to write about in your own Japanese Tanka poem.

How would you describe the place so someone reading or hearing your Tanka might see the same picture in their mind also? What colors do you see? What shapes and textures?

Are you thinking of a living creature? Or maybe a living creature traveling through a natural place or setting? As you write, help your reader see what you see using words.

Remember to use the 5/7/5 pattern of syllables! Share your Tanka with a friend, an adult you know, or a teacher!

Chapter 6 Thoughts

The mind is always thinking, even while you sleep. Our thoughts are our own. When writing poetry, poets share the thoughts in their minds.

Sometimes our thoughts move on their own. Sometimes we take charge of our thoughts. Poets take charge of their thoughts in creative ways. Poets use their imaginations.

Read these Tanka Poems created about thoughts.

Wondering

I wonder if I'll
get good grades ... I wonder what
I'll be when I grow
up ... I wonder if I'll be
a pro wrestler ... or a

book illustrator ...
I wonder if I'll own a
dog or a cat ... I
wonder if I'll ever run
faster than my brother ... I
wonder if I'll win the race

When I Grow Up

When I Grow Up I

want to be a vet you know,

a doctor for sick

animals so, if my dog,

Rosco, should catch a cold or

an ear infection

I will find a cure for him,

he will get better

then, we will live together

until we are very old

The Importance of Napkin Placement

Why should I place a

napkin on my lap if soups

and such dribble down

my chin falling onto my

shirt, because then I look down

to see drops landing

on my lap, so then I move

the napkin from my

lap to clean my mouth, my shirt

my mouth, and again, my lap

Johnny on the Spot

Johnny on the spot
they call me quick as a wink
that's me I'm on the
fly on a dime a flash but
not in the pan I'm on the

ball lickety-split
faster than greased lightening
or my bestie Speed
Racer I'm there in a heart
Beat of a New York minute

What is a thought going through your mind right now? Do you have a thought or idea you have been thinking about for a while? If you had a moment to daydream, what thoughts might run through your head?

Choose one of your thoughts to use in a Japanese Tanka poem. Once you begin writing, just let your thoughts take you wherever they want to go.

Try writing your own Thought Tanka poem. Remember to use the 5/7/5 pattern of syllables! Share your Haiku with a friend, an adult you know, or a teacher.

You have come to the end of your introduction to Kids Read and Write Japanese Tanka ... but this is not the end of creating new Tanka Poems!

You know how to recognize the pattern and write Japanese Tanka Poems so you can write a Japanese Tanka Poem on just about any subject!

Congratulations on becoming a poet of Japanese Tanka Poems!

Never stop learning and keep on writing!

About the Author

VA Rivera is a retired educator who loves poetry and laughing out loud. VA Rivera lives happily in Yonkers, New York with a gentle pastel calico named HoneyBun and a feisty Tiger Stripe named SweetiePie.

VA spent 30 years teaching children how to read and write different types of poems. Many class collections were published, and every child created a poetry journal to bring home and keep forever.

VA continues to write her own poetry that she workshops with a favorite online group of the most wonderful poets. VA encourages all children to read and write their own original poetry.

Share with me the Japanese Tanka poems you write! I would love to read your favorites!

Email me: va_rivera@varivera.com

Website: www.varivera.com

"If you read poems you will learn to understand poems. If you learn to understand poems, you will learn to love poetry."   VA Rivera